SUPER BOWL SUPERSTARS

TOM BRADY
and the
New England Patriots

SUPER BOWL XLIX

By K.C. Kelley

Consultant: James Buckley Jr.
Former Editor, *NFL Magazine*

BEARPORT
PUBLISHING

New York, New York

Credits

Cover and Title Page, © AP/Wide World/Kevin Terrell; 4, © Newscom/Larry W. Smith/EPA; 5, © Lionel Hahn/Abaca USA; 6, © Fotosports International; 7, © Courtesy San Mateo High School; 8, © Joe Robbins; 9, © Mike Jula; 10, © AP/Wide World/Al Messerschmidt Archive; 11, © Delane B. Rouse; 12, © Kevin Recce/Icon SMI; 13, © Lionel Hahn/KRT; 14, © SportsChrome; 15, © Mark Cornelison/MCT; 16, © Allen Eyestone/ZUMA; 17, © John Angelillo/UPI; 18, © Kevin Deitsch/UPI; 20, © Newscom/Larry W. Smith/EPA; 21, © Kevin Deitsch/UPI; 22 (bkgd.), © Kevin Deitsch/UPI; 22L, © Dick Druckman/ZUMA; 22R, © Erik K. Lesser/EPA.

Publisher: Kenn Goin
Editor: Jessica Rudolph
Creative Director: Spencer Brinker
Produced by Shoreline Publishing Group LLC

Library of Congress Cataloging-in-Publication Data in process at time of publication (2016)
Library of Congress Control Number: 2015017880
ISBN-13: 978-1-62724-869-3

For more information, write to Bearport Publishing Company, Inc., 45 West 21st Street, Suite 3B, New York, New York 10010. Printed in the United States of America.

10 9 8 7 6 5 4 3 2 1

☆ Contents ☆

What It Takes

Quarterback Tom Brady looked up at the clock. Just over 12 minutes were left in Super Bowl XLIX (49). Tom's team, the New England Patriots, trailed the Seattle Seahawks 24–14. The Seahawks had the best **defense** in the **NFL**. A Patriots **comeback** seemed almost impossible.

Tom had faced tough moments like this before. In fact, he had led the Patriots to many Super Bowls. However, did Tom still have what it takes to win another Super Bowl championship?

Tom Brady looks for an open teammate during Super Bowl XLIX (49), on February 1, 2015.

Tom (#12) calls out signals to his teammates during Super Bowl XLIX (49).

Super Bowl XLIX (49) was the eighth Super Bowl game the Patriots played. Only the Dallas Cowboys and the Pittsburgh Steelers have also played in that many Super Bowls.

Getting Started

Tom has always loved football. As a child, his dream was to be a pro quarterback like his hero, Joe Montana. However, Tom's parents wouldn't let him play much. They thought the game was too rough.

Fortunately, Tom's parents eventually changed their minds, and he quickly proved to be an incredible talent on the field. Tom's strong arm helped him become one of the top high school quarterbacks in the country. In three seasons, he threw 31 touchdown passes for his team.

Quarterback Joe Montana, Tom's hero, led the San Francisco 49ers to four Super Bowl wins.

Tom went to high school in San Mateo, California.

Tom also played on his high school baseball team, as a **catcher**. The Montreal Expos were so impressed with his skills that they **drafted** him. However, Tom decided to instead focus on football.

Almost Left Out

After high school, Tom got a **scholarship** to play football for the University of Michigan. He started as a **backup** for the Wolverines. In his junior year, though, he earned the **starting** quarterback position. He was so good that the next year, he led his team to victory in the **Orange Bowl**.

In 2000, Tom entered the NFL draft. At first, many teams passed him over. Finally, the New England Patriots chose him in the sixth round. Tom was excited and eager to prove how good he was.

Tom's childhood dreams came true when he joined the Patriots in 2000.

Tom (#10) playing for the
Michigan Wolverines

Bowl games, like the
Orange Bowl, are played after
the college football regular
season. Only the best college
football teams play in them.

The Young Champ

Tom spent his **rookie** season as the Patriots' backup quarterback. Then, in 2001, Tom got his chance. The starting quarterback for New England was hurt early in the season. Tom became the starter. With their new leader, the Patriots won 11 games in the regular season. Then they won the **AFC Championship Game**—and earned a trip to Super Bowl XXXVI (36).

During the Super Bowl, the St. Louis Rams tied the score with less than two minutes left. Tom stayed focused and guided his team into position for a game-winning **field goal**. The kicker nailed it! The Patriots won 20–17!

Tom played in only one regular-season game during his rookie year with the Patriots.

Tom (#12) throws a pass during Super Bowl XXXVI (36), on February 3, 2002.

After Super Bowl XXXVI (36), Tom was named the Super Bowl **MVP**. He was only 24 years old. At the time, he was the youngest MVP in Super Bowl history.

Top of the League

Over the next three seasons, the Patriots were the best team in the NFL. Tom's pinpoint passes were a big reason for their success. In the 2003 season, the Patriots reached Super Bowl XXXVIII (38). Tom threw three touchdown passes against the Carolina Panthers. This game also came down to a last-minute field goal. The ball sailed between the goal posts, and the Patriots became champs once again!

The next season, New England reached the Super Bowl—yet again. They beat the Philadelphia Eagles 24–21 to win Super Bowl XXXIX (39). The Patriots were on fire. It seemed like nothing could stop them.

Tom talks to a reporter after being named MVP of Super Bowl XXXVIII (38).

Tom prepares for a play during Super Bowl XXXVIII (38), on February 1, 2004.

Super Bowl XXXIX (39) was New England's third Super Bowl win in four years. New England was only the second team in NFL history to win three Super Bowls in four seasons. The first team was the Dallas Cowboys.

Disappointment

In the 2007 and 2011 seasons, Tom led the Patriots back to the Super Bowl. In Super Bowl XLII (42), the Patriots had the lead late in the game. However, New York Giants **wide receiver** David Tyree made an amazing catch. His play set up the Giants' game-winning touchdown pass.

A few years later, the Giants shocked the Patriots again in Super Bowl XLVI (46). New England led for most of the game. However, New York scored with less than a minute left, and won 21–17. Tom and his teammates were disappointed by these tough losses.

Tom sits on the sidelines during Super Bowl XLVI (46).

Receiver David Tyree (#85) made a great catch that helped New York beat New England 17–14 in Super Bowl XLII (42), on February 3, 2008.

In 2007, Tom set an NFL record by throwing 50 touchdown passes in the regular season. His record was broken in 2013 by Peyton Manning, who threw 55 touchdowns.

Another Try

Despite the losses, Tom continued to focus on helping his team achieve more victories. Under his leadership, the Patriots had won three Super Bowls—but they wanted even more. The 2014 season started out rough, though. The Patriots lost two of their first four games. Tom was now 37. Some fans wondered if he could play as well as he had when he was younger.

Tom didn't pay attention to these comments. After the season's slow start, he led his team on a seven-game winning streak. In the AFC Championship Game, New England beat the Indianapolis Colts 45–7. That meant Tom was going to the Super Bowl—for the sixth time!

Tom getting tackled early in the 2014 season

Tom threw three touchdowns to help the Patriots crush the Colts in the AFC Championship Game.

After the AFC Championship Game, some people said the Patriots had broken the rules. The NFL **investigated** and decided to punish Tom and his team for taking too much air out of the footballs used in that game.

Comeback King

In Super Bowl XLIX (49), New England faced a tough opponent, the Seattle Seahawks. The Seahawks had won the championship the year before. They had the best defense in the NFL—but the Patriots had the best quarterback. In the first half of the game, Tom threw two touchdown passes to tie the score. By the fourth quarter, however, the Seahawks had gained a 24–14 lead.

No team in Super Bowl history had ever come back from ten points down in the second half. Tom knew what he had to do. He led the Patriots on two long **drives** that ended in touchdowns.

Julian Edelman (#11) spikes the ball after catching a fourth-quarter touchdown pass from Tom.

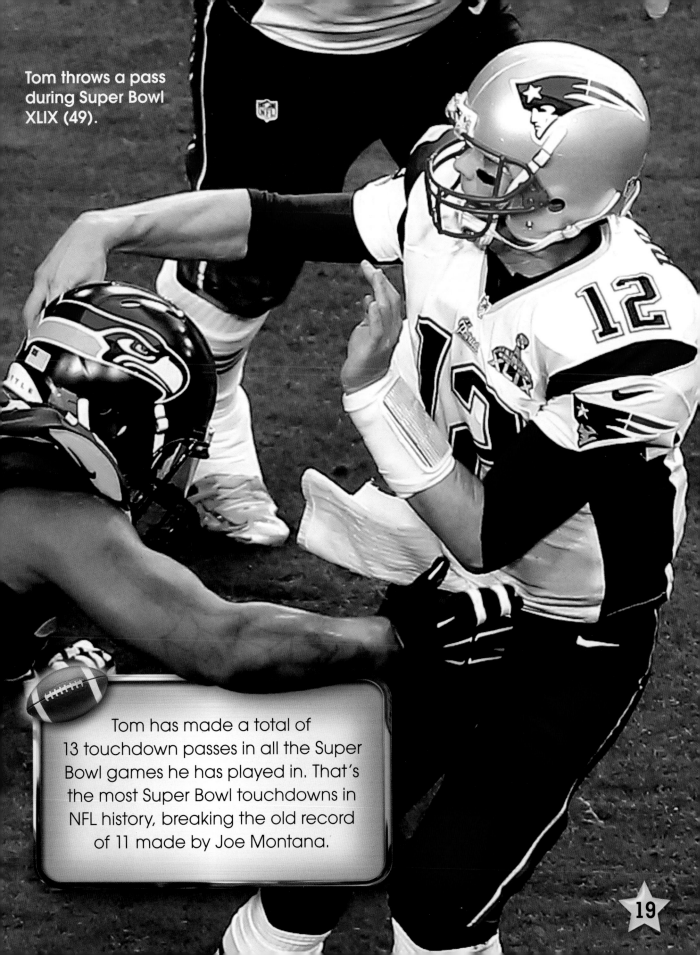

Tom throws a pass during Super Bowl XLIX (49).

Tom has made a total of 13 touchdown passes in all the Super Bowl games he has played in. That's the most Super Bowl touchdowns in NFL history, breaking the old record of 11 made by Joe Montana.

A Shocking Ending!

The Seahawks weren't done fighting for a win. In the final 20 seconds of the game, they reached the Patriots' one-yard line. Seattle tried to score on a pass, but Patriots **cornerback** Malcolm Butler **intercepted** it! The Patriots won the Super Bowl 28–24.

The Patriots and their fans were on top of the world. Tom joined Joe Montana and Terry Bradshaw as the only quarterbacks with four Super Bowl wins. Many consider Tom to be one of the greatest quarterbacks of all time.

Malcolm Butler (#21) intercepts a pass late in the game.

Tom celebrates another Super Bowl win with Patriots head coach Bill Belichick (right).

Tom was named the MVP of Super Bowl XLIX (49). He became the second player after Joe Montana to become a three-time Super Bowl MVP.

Key Players

There were other key players on the New England Patriots who helped win Super Bowl XLIX (49). Here are two of them.

Julian Edelman #11

Position: Wide receiver

Born: 5/22/86, Redwood City, California

Height: 5'10" (1.8 m)

Weight: 198 pounds (90 kg)

Key Plays: Made 9 catches for 109 yards (100 m)

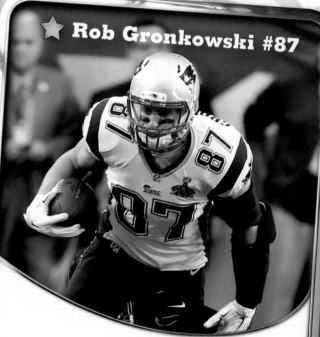

Rob Gronkowski #87

Position: Tight end

Born: 5/14/89, Amherst, New York

Height: 6'6" (2 m)

Weight: 265 pounds (120 kg)

Key Plays: Made 6 catches for 68 yards (62 m); his 22-yard (20 m) catch made Tom the all-time leader in Super Bowl touchdown passes

Glossary

AFC Championship Game (AY-EFF-SEE CHAM-pee-uhn-ship GAYM) a playoff game that decides which American Football Conference team will go to the Super Bowl against the winner of the NFC (National Football Conference) Championship Game

backup (BAK-uhp) a player who waits to replace another player at the same position

catcher (KACH-ur) a player in baseball who squats behind home plate and receives pitches from the pitcher

comeback (KUM-bak) a return to the lead in a game after a team had been behind

cornerback (KOR-nur-bak) a defensive player who usually covers the other team's receivers

defense (DEE-fens) the players on the field who try to stop the other team's offense

drafted (DRAFT-id) chosen at the event in which pro sports teams take turns selecting high school or college athletes to play for them

drives (DRYVES) in football, a series of plays that lead to a score

field goal (FEELD GOHL) a kicking play in football that is worth three points if done successfully

intercepted (in-tur-SEP-tid) caught a pass meant for a player on the other team

investigated (in-VESS-tih-gay-tid) looked at evidence to find an answer or a solution

MVP (EM-VEE-PEE) letters standing for Most Valuable Player, an award given to the best player in a game or in a season

NFL (EN-EFF-ELL) letters standing for the National Football League, the group of 32 teams that play pro football

Orange Bowl (OR-inj BOWL) a college football game played in January after the regular season

rookie (RUK-ee) a player in his or her first season in a pro sport

scholarship (SKOL-ur-ship) an award that helps pay for a person to go to college

starting (STAR-ting) being the coach's first choice to play in a game

wide receiver (WYDE ree-SEE-ver) a player whose job it is to catch passes

Bibliography

Bishop, Greg. "Elated." *Sports Illustrated* (February 4, 2015).

www.nfl.com/player/tombrady/2504211/profile

Official Site of the New England Patriots: www.patriots.com

Read More

Allen, Kathy. *Tom Brady (Football Stars Up Close)*. New York: Bearport (2013).

Scheff, Matt. *Tom Brady: Football Superstar (Superstar Athletes)*. North Mankato, MN: Capstone (2014).

Learn More Online

To learn more about Tom Brady, the New England Patriots, and the Super Bowl, visit **www.bearportpublishing.com/SuperBowlSuperstars**

Index